W9-APO-755

Disaster!

The Hindenburg

The Fiery Crash of a German Airship

by Kathleen W. Deady

Consultant:
Carl Jablonski
President
Navy Lakehurst Historical Society

CAPSTONE
HIGH-INTEREST
BOOKS

an imprint of Capstone Press
Mankato, Minnesota

Capstone High-Interest Books are published by Capstone Press
151 Good Counsel Drive, P.O. Box 669, Mankato, Minnesota 56002
http://www.capstone-press.com

Library of Congress Cataloging-in-Publication Data
Deady, Kathleen W.
    The Hindenburg: the fiery crash of a German airship/by Kathleen W. Deady.
    p. cm.—(Disaster!)
    Summary: Describes the giant airship "Hindenburg," the events that led up
to its explosive crash on a New Jersey airfield in 1937, and the effects of the
disaster on airship travel.
    Includes bibliographical references and index.
    ISBN 0-7368-1321-7 (hardcover)
    1. Hindenburg (Airship)—Juvenile literature. 2. Aircraft accidents—New
Jersey—Juvenile literature. [1. Hindenburg (Airship) 2. Airships. 3. Aircraft
accidents.] I. Title. II. Disaster! (Capstone High-Interest Books)
TL659.H5 D435 2003
363.12'465—dc21   2001008334

Editorial Credits
Matt Doeden, editor; Karen Risch, product planning editor; Kia Adams, designer;
    Jo Miller, photo researcher

Photo Credits
Bettmann/CORBIS, 10, 13, 18, 22
CORBIS, 14, 21
Hulton Archive by Getty Images, cover, 4, 6, 7, 25
Jack Dabaghian/Reuters/Timepix, 26–27
Mansell/Timepix, 9, 16

1 2 3 4 5 6 07 06 05 04 03 02

Table of Contents

Features

Fast Facts about the *Hindenburg*

Length: 804 feet (245 meters)

Width: 135 feet (41 meters)

Height: 147 feet (45 meters)

Weight: 242 tons (220 metric tons)

Total Hydrogen Gas Capacity: more than 7.6 million cubic feet (215,000 cubic meters)

Top Speed: 82 miles (132 kilometers) per hour

Year Built: 1936

Cost to Build: $3,750,000

Date Crashed: May 6, 1937

People Aboard: 97

Survivors: 62

The Disaster

On May 6, 1937, a giant airship called the *Hindenburg* floated over the New Jersey countryside. The huge ship, called a zeppelin, was nearing the end of a three-day voyage from Germany.

The ship had finished crossing the Atlantic Ocean earlier in the day. It had flown over Boston, Massachusetts, and New York City. Passengers and crew members prepared for the airship to land at Lakehurst Naval Air Station in New Jersey.

The Storm

The weather in New Jersey became stormy during the afternoon. Heavy rain fell at the air station. Max Pruss was the *Hindenburg's* commander. He decided that the ship should not land until the weather calmed.

The *Hindenburg's* route took it over several large U.S. cities.

Early in the evening, the rain slowed to a light drizzle. Pruss was ready to land. He lowered the *Hindenburg* to about 650 feet (200 meters) above the ground and guided it toward the air station.

Pruss slowed the ship as it neared the landing spot. He also vented some of the ship's gas, causing the ship to fall closer to the ground. Soon, the giant ship was less than 300 feet (90 meters) above the ground. It was 800 feet (244 meters) from the docking mast, where it would be tied to the ground. The crew dropped the first mooring ropes. Members of the ground crew below prepared to tie these ropes to the docking mast.

Count Ferdinand von Zeppelin was the first person to build an airship. His airship took its first flight in 1900.

Explosion

At 7:25 in the evening, the *Hindenburg* was 260 feet (79 meters) above the ground. Suddenly, a small flame burst from the rear of the ship. The hydrogen gas inside the *Hindenburg* exploded. Within seconds, almost half of the ship was burning.

The back end of the ship quickly sank. Flames spread toward the front. Soon, flames shot out of the ship's nose. The whole ship fell to the ground. Within 34 seconds, it was nothing but burning wreckage.

The People

The passengers and crew aboard the *Hindenburg* had to act quickly. In the first seconds, some people jumped or fell from the ship's windows. But the ship was still high in the air. Many of these people died.

Many people stayed on the ship as long as they could. Some of these people waited to jump until the ship was closer to the ground. Others slid down the mooring ropes to the ground. Some people waited too long and were killed by the fire or by the crash.

The ground crew quickly rushed to help. They found many survivors badly burned. They found many other people already dead.

A total of 36 people died as a result of the *Hindenburg* explosion. Of these people, 13 were passengers, 22 were crew members, and one was a member of the ground crew. One of the people who died was a 14-year-old girl. Two dogs aboard the *Hindenburg* also died.

The *Hindenburg* burst into flames as it attempted to land in New Jersey.

History and Design

The *Hindenburg* was the largest airship ever built. A German named Hugo Eckener designed and built the *Hindenburg*. Eckener became interested in airships around 1900. Airplanes were not being flown at this time. The only way to fly was with large hot-air balloons. Eckener imagined balloons that people could easily steer. He also imagined giant airships that could carry many passengers long distances.

The Early Years

In 1900, Eckener met Count Ferdinand von Zeppelin. Zeppelin also was interested in airships. He had recently invented the earliest design of an airship. Zeppelin's ship had a metal frame that held several balloons. He called these balloons "cells." He filled each cell with hydrogen. This gas is lighter than air. It caused the airship to rise.

Zeppelin added engines to his airship. He also added fins to steer the craft. His airship was called a dirigible, which means "able to be steered" in German.

Zeppelin tested his new craft in July 1900. Eckener watched the test flight. He was excited about Zeppelin's invention. Eckener soon joined Zeppelin's company to build more dirigibles.

The early dirigibles had many accidents. But Zeppelin and Eckener continued to test and improve them. Airship travel soon became safe and common. By 1914, more than 34,000 passengers had traveled by airship in Germany. People called the airships "zeppelins."

Zeppelin's airships had large metal frames.

Eckener's Dream

After Zeppelin died in 1917, Eckener became director of the company. In 1928, Eckener built the *Graf Zeppelin*. He flew this large zeppelin across the Atlantic Ocean to the United States. In 1929, he flew it around the

Crew members served meals to the *Hindenburg*'s passengers in the dining room.

world. He wanted to show the world that airship travel was safe and comfortable.

Eckener had even bigger ideas. He planned to build a whole fleet of airships. The first in the fleet would be called the *Hindenburg*. Eckener wanted it to be the perfect airship.

Eckener built the *Hindenburg* bigger and better than any airship before it. He finished building the ship in 1936. It measured 804 feet (245 meters) long. It was more than 135 feet (41 meters) wide. The ship's 16 cells held more than 7.6 million cubic feet (215,000 cubic meters) of hydrogen. Four 16-cylinder diesel engines powered the ship.

Some people described the *Hindenburg* as a floating hotel. The *Hindenburg's* great size allowed extra room for passengers. The passenger areas were located on two decks at the bottom of the ship. These decks spread all the way across the ship. The *Hindenburg* had a fancy dining room and lounges for people to look down at the ground below.

What Went Wrong

Millions of people in the United States listened to radio reports as the *Hindenburg* exploded. Newspapers around the world printed stories about the disaster. People became afraid to fly in zeppelins. Airship travel dropped quickly after the disaster.

Scientists and investigators studied the *Hindenburg* wreckage. They looked at photos of the explosion. They talked to people who had been aboard the ship. But the investigators could not figure out what caused the disaster. They could only guess.

Hydrogen Gas

The *Hindenburg* used hydrogen gas to float. Hydrogen is a flammable gas. It catches fire easily. The hydrogen in the *Hindenburg's* cells caused the flames to spread quickly.

When Eckener built the *Hindenburg,* he planned to use helium gas instead of hydrogen. Helium is not flammable. But Eckener could not afford to buy enough helium to lift the ship. He used hydrogen instead.

Investigators knew that something had set the hydrogen cells on fire. That was the only way the *Hindenburg* could have been destroyed so quickly. They searched for the cause of the fire.

Eckener was forced to use flammable hydrogen gas in the *Hindenburg* because he could not find enough affordable helium gas.

FAMOUS WORDS

Many news reporters had gathered in New Jersey to cover the landing of the *Hindenburg*. Herbert Morrison was one of these reporters. He covered the event for a radio station in Chicago, Illinois. His description of the events is one of the most famous radio broadcasts in history. Here are some of his words to describe the disaster:

"It burst into flames! Get out of the way! Get out of the way! . . . It's burning, bursting into flames and is falling on the mooring mast, and all the folks agree that this is terrible. This is the worst of the worst catastrophes in the world! Oh, it's crashing . . . oh, four or five hundred feet into the sky, and it's a terrific crash, ladies and gentlemen. There's smoke, and there's flames, now, and the frame is crashing to the ground, not quite to the mooring mast . . . Oh, the humanity, and all the passengers screaming around here!"

Possible Causes

The storm had not completely passed over New Jersey when the *Hindenburg* exploded. Many people guessed that lightning started the fire. But lightning had struck the *Hindenburg* many times before. It never had caused a problem.

Other people guessed that a spark of electricity started the fire. Wet mooring ropes could have carried a small electric charge from the ground. But investigators did not believe this idea. The mooring ropes were at the front of the ship. The fire had started in the ship's rear.

Some people thought that a passenger may have set off a bomb. The *Hindenburg* was a German ship. At that time, the German government was very unpopular with many groups. Some people thought a passenger may have blown up the ship to make the German government look bad. But the investigators found nothing in the wreckage that supported this idea.

The governments of both the United States and Germany searched for an answer. But they never found anything to prove what had caused the fire. The investigators agreed that the most likely cause was an electric spark, but they did not know where it came from.

Scientists and engineers performed many tests as they tried to learn what caused the *Hindenburg* explosion.

What We Have Learned

The *Hindenburg* disaster changed the way people thought about airships. Many people stopped traveling by airship. Companies built bigger and safer airplanes during the late 1930s and the 1940s. Soon, airplane travel completely replaced airship travel.

Recent Studies

Today, people still wonder what caused the fire aboard the *Hindenburg*. Many scientists and historians have thought of new ideas about the cause of the fire. But now, there is no way to prove what happened. The disaster probably will remain a mystery forever.

Retired NASA engineer Addison Bain wanted to know more about the *Hindenburg*. He studied the giant airship's design. He looked for possible causes that earlier investigators had not considered. In 1997, he published his studies about the disaster.

Bain believes the fire started with the cloth used to cover the outside of the *Hindenburg*. The cloth was covered with varnish. This clear coating made the cloth waterproof, but it also was highly flammable. Bain believes the varnish caught fire and caused the cloth to burn. The flames then spread to the cells that carried the ship's hydrogen.

People today still are not sure what started the fire aboard the *Hindenburg*.

Some companies today use airships as cargo ships and to display large advertisements.

The Effects Today

People still are interested in the *Hindenburg* disaster. Officials at the Navy Lakehurst Historical Society hold a service each year on May 6 at 7:25 in the evening. They remember those who died in the accident.

Recently, people have become interested in airships again. Several companies have studied safer ways to build them. These companies do not plan to use airships for passenger travel. Instead, they plan to carry cargo inside the ships. Other companies plan to use airships for military purposes. Airships have advantages over airplanes. They do not need large runways to take off and land. They are much quieter than airplanes, and they cause less pollution. In the future, airships may become common once again.

Timeline

Count Ferdinand von Zeppelin launches the first dirigible.

An airship called the *Graf Zeppelin* makes the first passenger trip across the Atlantic Ocean.

1900   **1914**   **1928**   **1929**

Airship travel becomes common in Germany.

The *Graf Zeppelin* flies around the world in 21 days.

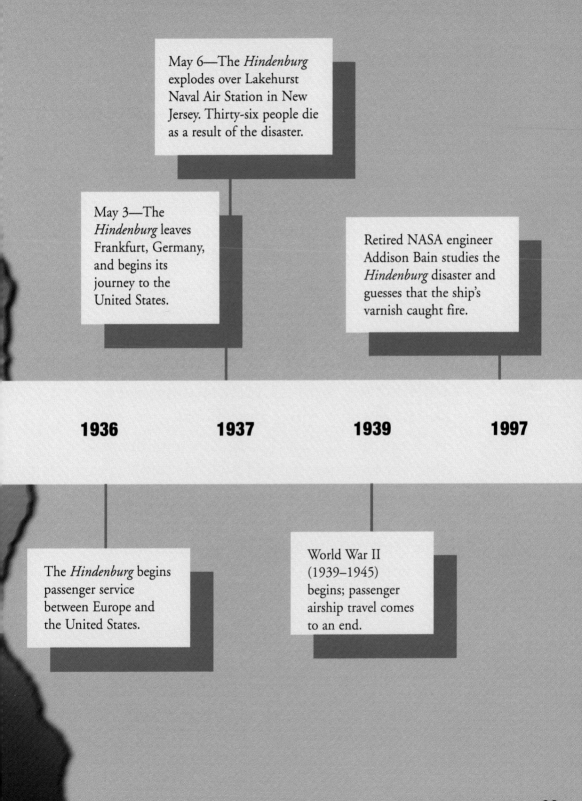

May 6—The *Hindenburg* explodes over Lakehurst Naval Air Station in New Jersey. Thirty-six people die as a result of the disaster.

May 3—The *Hindenburg* leaves Frankfurt, Germany, and begins its journey to the United States.

Retired NASA engineer Addison Bain studies the *Hindenburg* disaster and guesses that the ship's varnish caught fire.

1936 **1937** **1939** **1997**

The *Hindenburg* begins passenger service between Europe and the United States.

World War II (1939–1945) begins; passenger airship travel comes to an end.

Words to Know

dirigible (dihr-UH-juh-buhl)—an aircraft that is lighter than air and that can be steered

docking mast (DOK-ing MAST)—a tall pole that holds an airship to the ground

helium (HEE-lee-uhm)—a colorless, lightweight gas that does not burn

hydrogen (HYE-druh-juhn)—a colorless gas that is lighter than air and burns easily

mooring ropes (MOR-ing ROHPS)—ropes used to tie down a ship or aircraft

varnish (VAR-nish)—a clear coating that gives an object a shiny appearance

wreckage (REK-ij)—the broken remains of an object that has crashed

zeppelin (ZEP-lin)—a large oval-shaped airship with a rigid frame; zeppelins are named for their inventor, Count Ferdinand von Zeppelin.

To Learn More

DeAngelis, Gina. *The Hindenburg.* Great Disasters, Reforms and Ramifications. Philadelphia: Chelsea House, 2001.

O'Brien, Patrick. *The Hindenburg.* New York: Henry Holt, 2000.

Sherrow, Victoria. *The Hindenburg Disaster: Doomed Airship.* American Disasters. Berkeley Heights, N.J.: Enslow, 2002.

Useful Addresses

Canada Aviation Museum
Rockcliffe Airport
11 Aviation Parkway
P.O. Box 9724, Station T
Ottawa, ON K1G 5A3

Navy Lakehurst Historical Society
P.O. Box 328
Lakehurst, NJ 08733

Internet Sites

Fall of the Hindenburg
http://www.infoplease.com/spot/hindenburg1.html

Navy Lakehurst Historical Society—Hindenburg
http://www.nlhs.com/hindenburg.htm

Index